in white

volume i of a silent trilogy

by

Published by Untold Imprint
www.sdarling-art.com

ISBN: 978-1-7641672-0-8
Printed in: Australia

a minute of quiet disturbance
in a loud and shouting world

this is a collection of moments
written and experienced over fourteen years—
some through clarity,
others through the strange distance
of a world that often felt unreal.
not in order,
not in narrative,
but as fragments
shaped by silence,
tension,
and reflection.

in white is the first of three.
this is not a story.
it is a pause between two thoughts.
you are not asked to understand it.
only to drift along its edges,
and listen between its lines.

this is not just a book.
it is an experience
meant to be absorbed,
not explained.

i. whispers

all she sought
was never enough—
no energies,
no flash.

she searched
for adventures and stories—
the kind of girl
you want to get lost in.

some might not want to be loved
as much as understood.

i wanted to learn about her past—
not to punish her,
but to understand
how she needs to be loved.

the problem isn't
what you're feeling;

it's what you're letting yourself think
because of what you feel.

a deep conversation,
unfamiliar scenery,
a beautiful mind
and a vivid soul—

this is
a new way
of making love.

she is not meant to be solved,
but witnessed—
a collision of softness and storm,
held together
by nothing but will.

there is no map
for a mind like hers—
only the quiet privilege
of getting lost inside it.

in her presence,
there is a stillness
that undresses the soul.

no words,
no choreography—
just the electricity
of being seen.

desire,
not as fire,
but as warmth
that lingers
in the space between breaths.

i no longer chase the summit.

what i seek
is to stand where my feet are—
to find stillness
in the space between striving.

somewhere in the small,
i found the vast—
and i have never felt freer.

the soul doesn't rush.

it waits
at the edge of every decision,
asking only one thing—

will this bring you home,
or take you further away?

sometimes the soul speaks
in a voice
the mind can't follow.

so it paints in dreams,
bleeds through the fingertips,
and waits—
until you're quiet enough
to hear.

i walked into the dark,
not to escape the light—

but to see
if i could still glow
without anyone watching.

in the stillness
before the noise begins,
when the world feels like a held breath,
i hope you feel the weight
of being alive.

not the sweetness,
but the strangeness.
the invisible gravity
that keeps you tethered
to something unnamed.

some mornings arrive
like ghosts—
not asking to be understood,
only witnessed.

in those hours,
you may find
that peace is not the absence of pain,
but the presence of something
more ancient than joy.

a remembering.
a quiet agreement
between your breath
and the world
not to run.

and maybe,
if you stay still long enough,
you'll feel it—
the soft pull
toward what is real,
what is yours,
what is white.

not everything
feels like something else.

some experiences
defy comparison—
emotions
that can't be neatly categorized,
sensations
that elude description.

in the vast landscape
of human perception,
there are nuances and subtleties
that words alone can't hold—
feelings
that transcend language.

and yet,
we try to understand the unfamiliar
by likening it to the familiar—
comparing it
to what we already know,
in an attempt
to make sense of the unknown.

but in doing so,
we risk oversimplifying
the complexity of our experience,
overlooking
the unique beauty
of each moment as it unfolds.

not everything
feels like something else.
and maybe
that's how it should be.

because in the mystery
and in the uncertainty—
we find
the true richness
of life.

close your eyes,
and let the words
paint you pictures—
each a brushstroke
upon the canvas of your mind,
a mesh
woven from the threads of thought.

for in the darkness
behind closed lids
lies a world
unbound by the constraints
of time and space—
where imagination soars
on wings
of whispered syllables.

let the colors dance.
let the scenes unfold
like petals opening
to the kiss of dawn—
revealing landscapes
of infinite possibility,
each stroke
a doorway
to another realm.

in the silence
of this shared communion,
let us wander together
through the gallery of the mind—
exploring the vast expanse
of human experience,
one word at a time.

i hope you find
a soft place to land—
a gentle refuge
in the storm of life,
where the harsh winds of reality
are tempered
by the warmth of compassion.

in the tumult of your journey,
may you discover
a sanctuary amidst the chaos—
a haven
where your weary soul
can find solace
and renewal.

i know the weight of the world
rests heavy upon your shoulders.
the burden of your sorrow
bears down
upon your fragile heart.

but in the darkness of despair,
i offer you
this flicker of hope—
a whispered prayer for peace,
and a wish
for your pain to ease.

so as you navigate
the rough terrain of existence,
may you stumble
upon a soft place to land.
and may it be
a beacon of light
in the shadowed landscape
of your sorrow.

the silence taught me
how to love emptiness.

not as lack—
but as a peaceful space
where the soul
has room to echo.

in that quiet,
nothing demanded an answer.
there were no clocks,
no names,
no edges to hold onto—
only the slow exhale
of being without performance.

i stopped needing to fill it.
i stopped apologizing for stillness.

and somewhere
in that quiet expanse,
i met myself
for the first time
without noise.

ii. within

to truly understand another,
we must immerse ourselves
in the depths of their experiences—
even the ones
that brought them to their knees.

it's about empathizing
with their struggles,
feeling the currents
of their emotions,
and navigating
the turbulent waters
that shaped their journey.

only by swimming
in the same waters
can we begin to see
the complexities of their soul—
and appreciate
the depth of their resilience.

there are rooms inside me
i only enter in silence.

they have no doors,
only echoes—

and somewhere in the distance,
my truest self
is still waiting
with open arms.

sometimes i disappear.
not to be missed,
but to remember
what it feels like
to exist
without being perceived—

to be real,
even when no one
is looking.

i am both—
a paradox in human form,
a synthesis of opposites,
a union of contradictions.
a blend of light and darkness,
of joy and sorrow,
of strength and vulnerability,
of chaos and order.

in the depths of my being,
i contain multitudes—
a complex tapestry
of experience and emotion,
woven into the fabric of my existence.

and yet,
ever-changing,
ever-evolving.

i am the creator
and the destroyer,
the architect of my destiny—
yet subject
to the whims of fate,
a mere actor
on the stage of life.

i am both the question
and the answer,
the seeker and the sought,
the student and the teacher.

for in the pursuit of knowledge,
i discover
i am both
the knower
and the known.

and so i embrace
the duality of my nature—
the contradictions
that define me.

because it is in the synthesis of opposites
that i find
harmony
and balance.

i am both—
and yet,
i am more.

a reflection
of the infinite possibilities
that lie within the human soul,
and the boundless potential
of existence.

there are things
i had to let die—
not because they were wrong,
but because they no longer
made room
for who i was becoming.

fall in love
with the world in me—
not the surface,
but the shadows beneath.
the places unnamed,
where silence hums
and memory folds in on itself.
where longing wears no name,
and truth is neither kind
nor cruel—
only still.

there is no map.
only dim corridors
and half-formed echoes.
but if you walk long enough,
if you let the dark speak first,
you'll find the rooms
i never meant to hide—
only forgot how to unlock.

come closer—
not to understand,
but to dissolve.
in the hush between breaths,
light gathers
in ways only the dark
could teach.

find the one
who understands your silence—

a whispered wisdom
passed down through the ages,
a reminder
that true connection
transcends the need for words.

for what is silence
but a language
spoken in the spaces between breaths,
in the echoes
of the heart's deepest desires,
in the unspoken truths
that linger in the air?

in the embrace
of the one who understands,
there is a sanctuary—
a refuge from the noise
and chaos of the world,
a haven
where the soul finds solace.

so let us seek out
those rare souls
who can hear
the whispers of our hearts,
who can decipher
the language of our silence—

and who,
in their presence,
make us feel
truly known
and understood.

i didn't lose myself.
i placed pieces of me
in safe places—

tucked beneath silence,
behind the walls i built
when i was too tired
to explain
what i was carrying.

some were folded into books
no one thought to open.
others buried
in the pauses between words
i wanted to say
but never did.

and now,
i spend my quiet days
gathering them back
without apology—

gently unfolding
the version of me
that waited patiently
to be remembered.

some truths
don't strike.
they slip—
like breath
beneath a closed door,
or a shadow
that doesn't move
when you do.

they wait
in the still places,
where no one looks—
not because they hide,
but because they know
you're not ready
to see.

and when they arrive,
they don't speak.
they exhale—
and suddenly,
the air
feels cleaner.

you are a terribly real thing
in a terribly false world—
a paradox
in the pattern of existence,
an inspiration of authenticity
in a sea of illusion

a reminder
of the power of truth
in the face of deception.

in the shadows of falsehood,
you shine like a star—
a guiding light in the darkness,
a testament
to the resilience of the human spirit,
and the capacity
for genuine connection
amidst the chaos.

in a world of masks
and facades,
you remain unapologetically yourself—
a rare gem
in a sea of imitation,
a living reminder
of the beauty of authenticity.

though the world may try
to bend you,
to mold you
into something you are not—
you stand firm
in your truth.

a monument
to the power
of the human soul.

so let us celebrate
your existence.

and embrace the reality
of who you are—
for in a world of falsehoods
and pretense,
you are a beacon of light,
shining brightly
for all to see.

sometimes memory
doesn't ask permission.

it arrives
like mist
rolling in
over calm water—

changing the shape
of everything
before you realize
you've already
stepped inside it.

the quieter i become,
the more i hear.

in the stillness of my soul,
amidst the hush,
the whispers of truth
echo in the silence—
revealing insights
that elude the noise.

as the world fades
into the background,
and the clamor
of everyday life subsides,
i attune myself
to the subtle rhythms of existence,
and the wisdom they carry.

in the absence of distraction,
my senses sharpen.
i become aware
of the nuances of life,
and the interconnectedness
of all things—

as if the universe itself
is speaking.

in this quiet communion
with the cosmos,
i find solace,
understanding,
and a peace
that transcends words.

for it is in the silence
that we find truth—
and in the stillness
that we find wisdom.

so i embrace the quiet,
and listen.
because it is in the listening
that we truly hear.

in the vast expanse of existence,
remember this truth—
you don't have to belong
everywhere.

in your youth,
you may feel the pull
to fit into every mold,
every role.

but the tapestry of life
has spaces undefined—
places to roam,
unshackled,
unconfined.

embrace your uniqueness.
let your spirit unfold.

in the beauty of diversity,
we find our place—
in the mosaic of humanity,
each with our own grace.

so wander freely.
explore the realms unknown.

belonging is found
in the heart you've sewn.

you don't have to belong
everywhere.
it's true.

just be yourself—
and the right spaces
will find you.

it's not about you anymore.

the realization
dawns
in quiet moments
of introspection—

when the focus shifts
from self
to something greater,
and the boundaries
of individuality
begin to blur.

for too long,
the world may have revolved
around your desires,
your ambitions,
your struggles.

but now,
in the clarity of understanding,
you see
the interconnectedness
of all things.

it's not about you anymore.

it's about
the collective journey—
the impact
we have on each other,
in ways both seen
and unseen.

and in this realization,
there is freedom—
a release
from the chains of ego
and self-interest.

a recognition
of the quiet,
inherent value
of every soul
that walks this earth.

so let go
of the need for validation.
let go
of the quest for personal glory.

and embrace
the beauty
of being part
of something
larger
than yourself.

i watched my past
drift away
like fog.

not erased—
just no longer needed
to see clearly.

i forgave myself
in the middle of a storm.

not because i was ready,
but because the wind
kept whispering—
you can't keep carrying this.

there are places inside me
no light reaches.

but they are not dead—
only resting,

waiting for the soft tap
of presence
to awaken them
without force.

iii. wrought

sometimes it's not the memory
that haunts you,
but the version of you
that didn't yet know
how it would all end—
and survive
anyway.

death brushed past me
once.

it said nothing—
just looked at me
like it already knew
how tightly i was holding
what was never mine
to keep.

i've seen the void.
it didn't swallow me.
it listened.

and in that quiet,
i realized—
the void only echoes
what we're too afraid
to admit.

i stared at the void
until it blinked.

it didn't speak—
but it noticed me,
and i noticed
that it had edges.

i had always imagined
it as endless,
but it wasn't.

it was shaped
by what i brought to it—
fear,
doubt,
memory.

and in that moment,
i understood:

even darkness flinches
when met without fear.
even the void,
for all its silence,
is waiting
to be seen
as something other than
absence.

the darkness never promised
safety—
only truth.

and truth,
when held gently,
is never cruel.

it just asks
to be seen
without the need
to be fixed.

i've met shadows
that felt kinder
than some hands.

and i've learned—
not all darkness
is cruel.

some just teaches
in a quieter voice.

there was a version of me
that lived only in mirrors.

i smiled,
but my eyes were rehearsed.

i buried myself
quietly—
and in that stillness,
i saw myself
for the first time.

at the bottom of my despair,
there was a door
i had never noticed.

it didn't lead out—
it led inward.

and what i found there
wasn't ruin,
but the softest
kind of rebirth.

i thought i had shattered.

but the pieces weren't broken—
just rearranged
in a way that made more sense
to the soul
i was becoming.

i lost parts of myself
on purpose.

they were never mine—
just survival masks
i forgot to take off
when the danger was gone.

we're not fleeing our darkness.
we're learning
to embrace it—
to love ourselves
within its depths.

i buried an old version of myself
in a place
no map remembers.

but sometimes,
in the hush before a storm,
i still hear my traces
moving through the silence.

even the stars burn out.

but the space they leave behind
is where new constellations form.

you are allowed
to go dark
for a while.

some nights i dissolve.
not from sadness—
but from detaching
everything that isn't real.

and in that weightlessness,
i remember:
i was never meant to stay whole,
only honest.

not every light is gentle.

some truths arrive
like shattered glass
under bare feet—

but even the blood
becomes part
of the cleansing.

pain doesn't vanish
when you outrun it—
it just changes shape,
waiting in corners
you haven't swept.

so i stopped.
i gave it stillness,
offered it presence.

and in that silence,
it loosened its grip,
and became something
almost tender.

in the midst
of life's tumultuous stream,
a sudden moment gleams—
truth,
bold and bare,
dispels the shadows
we clung to.

in an instant,
the veils fall.
no more hiding
behind gentle lies.

we stand,
hearts exposed,
navigating the storm
without illusion.

and somehow,
in that unexpected clarity,
we find the courage
to live
without turning away.

truth doesn't arrive
with permission—
but it does
set us free.

at the center
of every dark corner
of our unraveling selves
is a question
we never dared to ask.

and sometimes,
not fixing it,
not naming it—
just sitting beside it
is the answer.

let it fall apart.
let every fragile layer
shatter.

what's meant to remain
doesn't need your grip—
only your permission.

i walked so far
into myself
i stopped recognizing
the milestones.

nothing familiar—
just echoes,
and a strange kind of warmth
that whispered,

you've been here before
in dreams
you forgot.

the part of me
that wanted to run
was never afraid
of the world—

only afraid
that it wouldn't be allowed
to return
unchanged.

iv. wakes

i dream i'm falling,
just before i hit the ground—
a visceral plunge into the depths,
weightless.

the descent,
a cascade through the corridors of doubt,
each fleeting thought
a falling star
in the vast expanse.

before the impact,
a metamorphosis occurs;
wings unfold,
born of the dream's alchemy.

i ascend,
defying gravity's stern decree,
into the boundless sky
where silence reigns.

the dream—
a paradoxical journey of the psyche,
a descent into vulnerability,
a flight to liberation.

in the throes of falling,
i confront the unknown.
yet soaring upward,
i find solace in the infinite.

ground and sky—
two realms intertwined
in the dream's chiaroscuro,
where life's dichotomy unfolds.

the fall
is a prelude to a higher ascent—
a cyclical dance
between earthbound
and ethereal.

i dream of words
spoken into infinite space—
a poetic reverie
echoing through the cosmos,
each syllable
a starburst of meaning,
expanding outward
into the vast unknown.

in the silence of the void,
my voice resonates;
a whisper
carried on the cosmic winds
as i cast my thoughts
into the abyss
and watch them
dance among the stars.

for in the emptiness of space,
there is potential—
a canvas upon which
to paint the tapestry of existence.

with each word i speak,
i shape the universe,
molding reality
with the power
of imagination.

but amidst the infinite expanse,
i am but a speck—
a fleeting moment
in the grand symphony of creation.

and yet,
in my dreams,
i am infinite—
a boundless soul
reaching out
to touch the stars.

so let me dream
of words
spoken into infinite space,
and may my voice
echo through the cosmos—
a testament
to the power
of human imagination,
and the limitless
possibilities of the universe.

grief is a doorway
you don't walk through—
you dissolve into it.

and somehow,
on the other side,
you find a version of yourself
that understands beauty
in new ways.

time is not linear
inside the soul.

it folds inward,
replaying echoes,
rewriting meaning,
healing things
long after they've broken.

at the edge of the world,
where the sky kissed the earth
in a celestial embrace,
i found my liberation.

watching the stars burn out,
their cosmic elegy
became the backdrop
to my emancipation—
a poignant symphony of freedom
painted across
the canvas of the universe.

as the world tenderly embraced
its final curtain,
a bittersweet serenity washed over—

and in the gentle release
of earthly ties,
there emerged
a poignant beauty—
a sentiment of freedom
that fluttered
like ethereal wings,

carrying the spirit
to an expanse unbound
by the constraints
of the fading world.

in the deep recesses
where shadows converge,
there's something about silence
only the forest knows—

an enigma whispered
through rustling leaves,
as if nature guards secrets
within its wooded coves.

in the hush,
where echoes of solitude prevail,
a tale is woven
by the ancient trail.

silent footfalls
of creatures unseen, unheard,
a clandestine symphony—
the forest's whispered word.

the trees, silent sentinels,
bear witness to the unseen,
in the quiet of the woods,
where secrets convene.

a cryptic pact
between branches
and mossy floor—

the forest knows
of sorrows and untold delights,
in the depths of quiet,
where day surrenders to night.

in that stillness,
an arcane language
nature bestows—
there's something about silence
only the forest knows.

in the stillness of introspection,
i found clarity—
untangling the knots
of uncertainty
with sincerity.

with each revelation,
a weight lifted from my soul,
a metamorphosis unfolding,
making me whole.

no longer shackled
by the chains of the past,
i emerge reborn
from shadows cast.

a new version of myself,
head held high,
in a new mode,
ready to reach
for the sky.

gone are the doubts
that once clouded my mind,
replaced
by a sense of purpose,
clearly defined.

with newfound strength,
i stride forward—bold,
embracing the journey
as stories unfold.

in the crucible of transformation,
i see
the power of change
setting my spirit free.

with head held right
and heart aligned,
i embrace the dawn
of a new state of mind.

love is an ancient tension—
a strange chemistry
of gravity and silence,
pulling two bodies
into orbit,
then apart.

it is not softness,
but pressure—
the force that shapes stone
and fractures it.

a quiet war
of wanting to be known
without surrender.

not a tapestry,
but a fault line—
where longing meets resistance,
and belonging
is something
you earn
by staying
when it's easier to leave.

i'm becoming something else—
not fixed,
not whole,
just more true
than before.

your hands were kind,
but this ruin
was never yours to rebuild.

in the broken architecture
of my past,
i find the blueprints
etched in ash—
shapes only fire
could reveal.

this is not healing.
this is becoming.
alone,
unwatched,
i shed
what was never real.

let me vanish
and reappear
in a form
you won't recognize—
not better,
not worse,
but mine.

some things
i only see
with my eyes closed—
in the darkness
of my inner world,
where the boundaries
of reality blur
and the veil
of perception lifts.

in the depths of meditation,
i find clarity.
my mind's eye opens
to the mysteries
beyond the physical,
beyond the confines
of the mundane.

here,
in the realm of imagination,
i am free
to explore the recesses
of my soul—
to confront the truths
that elude me
in the harsh light of day.

for it is in the silence
of my own mind
that i find answers
to life's deepest questions—
and uncover
the wisdom within,
waiting
to be embraced.

so let me
close my eyes
and journey inward—
to the place
where truth and illusion
collide.

where the mysteries
of the universe
reveal themselves
in all their splendor.

if i had to recall
all the tough days,
i'd do it all again—
each painful step,
each shadowed hour
that tested my resolve.

for in the crucible
of suffering,
i found the strength
that forged
my fragile soul.

what is life
but a series of trials?
each moment,
a teacher.
each pain,
a guide.

in the darkness,
we discover our light.
through despair,
we glimpse
the threads of hope.

to relive hardship
is to know its worth—
to understand
the lessons carved
in grief,
the silent wisdom
hidden in tears,
the resilience
born from pain endured.

so,
i embrace the darkness
and the scars.
they shaped
the person
i've become.

in the echo
of those hard days,
i find
a testament
to the enduring spirit.

"i got a story worth telling,"
she declares—
her voice
a beacon
in the darkness of doubt.

a testament
to the power of resilience
in the face
of life's quiet wars.

for what is a story
but a journey
through the labyrinth
of human experience—
a tapestry
woven from joy
and sorrow,
triumph
and defeat?

in the telling,
she finds solace—
a balm
for past wounds,
a torch
to light the path ahead
through shadowed uncertainty.

but her story
is not hers alone.

it is a mirror
of the universal struggle—
the search
for meaning
in the chaos
of existence.

so let her speak.
let her words
echo through
the chambers of the heart.

and may they remind us—
our stories, too,
are worth telling.

"i wrote this march 21,"
a declaration
etched in the annals of time—
a marker of existence
in the ceaseless flow
of moments past.

for what is a date
but a signpost
along the winding road
of memory?
a reminder
of the passage of time,
and the ever-changing nature
of our lives.

in the ink-stained pages
of history,
each date holds a story—
a fragment
of the grand tapestry
of human experience.

a snapshot
captured
in the lens of time.

so let this
march 21
be more than a mark
on the calendar.

let it be
a testament
to the power of words
to transcend time—
to echo through the ages,
and touch the hearts
of those
yet to come.

i stood
at the edge of meaning,
and nothing answered.

no voice.
no sign.

just the vast,
pulsing quiet
of my own becoming—

and for once,
that was enough.

i thought the breaking
was the end.

but beneath the ruin
was a softer ground—
not failure,
but a return
to the part of me
that never needed saving.

sometimes,
i vanish from my life
just long enough
to remember—

i am not what i do.
i am the quiet
behind it.

we're not seeking
escape from our darkness.

we're striving
to find acceptance
and self-love
within its depths.

it's about embracing
our shadows
as integral parts
of who we are—
and discovering
the beauty
in our complexity.

through self-compassion,
we navigate the dark
with resilience
and grace,
finding strength
in our vulnerability
and authenticity.

never enough time
to do all the nothing
we want to do—

a paradox of life,
where moments slip
like sand
through open hands,
and idle dreams
remain
forever just.

in seeking meaning,
we fill our days
with tasks—
yet in the quiet spaces,
joy resides.

the simple act of being,
unconfined,
unrushed
by the demands
of fleeting time.

what is the worth of time
if not to breathe,
to feel the pulse of life
in every beat,
to savor silence,
and embrace the void—
finding fulfillment
in the unfilled hours?

so let us cherish
moments of pure stillness,
where doing nothing
becomes a sacred art.

and in that space,
discover life's true essence—
the beauty
of existence
unadorned.

i used to pray
for answers.

now i pray
for peace
with not knowing.

it's quieter here—
but somehow
more whole.

the soul doesn't rise
in fire.

it rises
in silence.

ashes are not the end—
they're a soft beginning
for things
too sacred
to be born in noise.

there was a silence
so complete
it felt like death—

until i realized
i could still feel
myself breathing.

that was the moment
i understood
rebirth.

there are truths
you can only hear
when everything else
has stopped
wanting something from you.

that's what solitude is—
not loneliness,
but sacred stillness
without obligation.

v. wanders

in a dream,
i watched myself
float away—

not dying,
just detaching
from everything
that had ever convinced me
i was small.

dreams
mixed with a little reality—
the best i ever had.

a fusion
of the ethereal and the concrete,
where imagination
dances with truth.

in the mess of life,
dreams
add hues to the mundane,
transforming the ordinary
into something extraordinary—
infusing moments
with a touch of magic.

yet reality grounds us,
keeps us tethered,
reminding us
that dreams alone
cannot sustain
what the soul
yearns to hold.

it is in the blending
that true beauty lies—
the delicate balance
between what is
and what could be.

the interplay
of light and shadow,
of fantasy
and fact.

for in this alchemy
of existence,
we find meaning,
purpose,
and possibility.

and in the blend
of dreams and reality,
we discover
the richness
of life itself.

and some memories
never leave.
they linger
like ghosts
in the corridors of our minds—
haunting us
with their presence,
refusing
to fade into the shadows.

in the tapestry
of our lives,
they are the threads
that bind the past
to what's yet to come—
shaping us
in ways
we do not always comprehend.

even as time
marches forward,
these memories remain
frozen in amber—
a testament
to the weight
of human experience.

though they may bring
pain or sorrow,
they remind us
of resilience—
of the spirit's ability
to endure.

so let us honor them.
for they are the keepers
of our truth,
the guardians
of the soul,
guiding us
through the journey
of life.

in the end,
we all just become stories—
narratives woven
into the fabric of time.
threads of existence,
intertwined
in the tapestry
of human experience.

each life
a chapter,
each moment
a verse—
a story of triumph
and tragedy,
of love
and loss,
of joy
and sorrow,
written in the ink
of our own deeds.

but what becomes
of these stories
when we are no longer
here to tell them—
when our voices
fall silent,
and our pens
run dry?

do we live on
in the echoes
of our tales,
passed down
through generations?
or do we fade
into obscurity,
forgotten
in the passage of time?

perhaps the answer
lies not in the stories themselves,
but in the impact
they leave behind—
in the hearts and minds
of those who hear them,
and the lessons
they carry forward.

for in the end,
it is not the length
of our stories
that matters,
but the depth
of their meaning—
and the legacy
we leave behind
in the lives
we've touched.

don't take too long
to notice the light—
it does not wait.
it burns through fog
and still,
we keep our eyes closed,
as if the dark owes us comfort.

hope doesn't knock.
it watches from a distance,
tired of proving it exists.
sometimes
it leaves
before you remember
it was ever there.

we grow addicted
to the weight in our heads,
the noise that numbs,
the familiar ache
of self-made storms.

but light—
it's never soft.
it splits you open
when you least expect it.
and if you look too late,
you might find
nothing left
but the shadow
of what it could have healed.

"i don't believe in yesterday,"
she said—
a whisper
in the winds of time.

a declaration
of defiance
against the weight
of history's relentless grip.

for what is yesterday
but shadows
cast upon the canvas
of memory?

phantoms
haunting the corridors
of thought,
whispers of a past
that cannot
be undone.

and yet—
even as we turn
our gaze forward,
yesterday's echoes
linger.

a faint reminder
of paths we've trod,
of choices made,
of roads
not taken.

but in this moment,
we stand
at the brink
of infinite possibility—

unbound
by what has been,
free
to write our own story,
unencumbered
by the ghosts
of regret.

in the dim corridors
of contemplation,
where thought unravels
like smoke in still air—

the first fracture appears.

not a revelation,
but a haunting.
a question
that never wanted
to be answered.

here,
in the far reaches of mind,
reality bleeds
into suggestion.

the veil between what is
and what could never be
grows thin.

what if truth
was just another illusion—
a safer name
for the unknown?

and still,
the questions circle
like crows.
not seeking answers,
but silence
to nest in.

what are we—
constructs of memory,
or architects of fate?

each thought
a step deeper
into a forest
with no path,
no light,
no promise of return.

but within that descent,
something ancient stirs—
a presence
that doesn't speak,
but watches.

for it is knowledge
we find
in the darkness—
when all else
has fallen away,
and we finally
recognize ourselves
by the quiet
light within.

i reach the end,
not with certainty,
but with the silence
that follows
a final breath.

ink dries slowly,
as if reluctant
to leave the page,

and i wonder
if the words
ever belonged
to me at all.

m.d.p

h.f

b.s.n.c

k.c

s.e

c.f.k

m.m

c.c.c

x.k

in the in-between
there is a middle place
where nothing thrives

in grey
follows next

STARLING

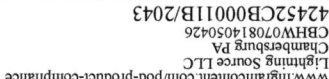